Jacqueline Farmer

Apples

Illustrated by Phyllis Limbacher Tildes

Charlesbridge

Few fruits are as beautiful, as colorful, or as healthful as the apple. Pretty to look at and a treat to eat, apples are the most popular fruit in the United States.

Granny Smith

McIntosh

Red Delicious

Growing apples

Along with many other fruits, apples are members of the rose family of plants. Apples are grown on farms known as orchards.

Apple trees are rarely grown from seeds. Trees grown from seeds do not always produce the same fruit as their parent tree. So to grow trees of a specific variety, farmers use a process called grafting. This is how it works:

Farmers choose a rootstock and a scion (SIE-un). The rootstock is the root of a young apple tree. The root determines the tree's size, life span, and resistance to pests and cold weather.

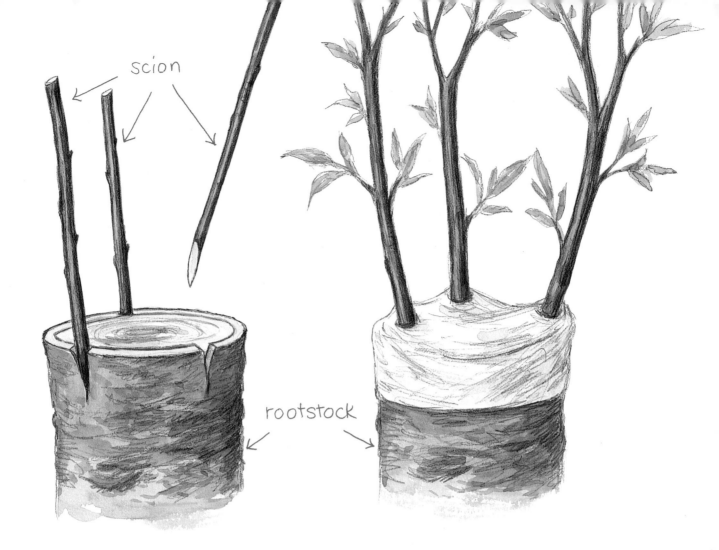

The scion is a sprout or bud that will become the branches that bear the apple tree's fruit. The scion also determines the apple tree's variety. Farmers insert a sprout of the apple variety they want to grow into the top of the rootstock. The rootstock can be of any variety. This process is called grafting.

For example, to grow Gala apples, scions from mature Gala apple trees must be grafted into the top of each rootstock. As a result these trees will produce only Gala apples.

As young apple trees grow, they must be pruned
and fertilized. Pruning means cutting out dead wood and
thinning out some of a tree's branches. Allowing extra
sunlight to reach the center of a tree helps the leaves and
apples grow. Fertilizer ensures that trees have the food
they need to be healthy.

Most apple trees must be four or five years old before
they are mature enough to produce fruit. Dwarf varieties,
which are small, can produce apples in the second season
after planting.

Apple trees grow best in cool areas. In winter they become dormant, which means the trees stop growing until spring.

When spring breezes warm the air, buds that line the mature apple trees' branches burst open. As the leaves unfold, farm workers apply an oil spray. This oil is safe for the trees but smothers insect eggs so that they do not hatch and damage the new fruit. The apple trees' pink-and-white flower blossoms fill the air with an amazing fragrance.

An apple blossom has both male and female parts.
The female part is the pistil, which includes the stigma
and ovary. The male part is the stamen, which makes the
pollen. As with many other fruits, an apple blossom doesn't
fertilize itself. In order for an apple to grow, pollen from
a different variety of apple tree must fertilize the flower.
This is called cross-pollination.

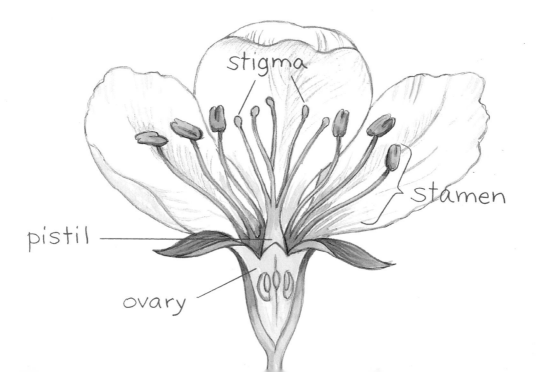

Pollen is spread either by the wind or by honeybees.
Apple farmers set up beehives in their orchards, and some
of them even rent extra hives to ensure good fertilization.

Busy honeybees collect nectar (a sweet liquid made by
flowers) and pollen from the blossoms. As they work they
carry the pollen from flower to flower and tree to tree.
Some of that pollen falls onto a blossom's stigma (the
sticky top of the pistil).

The pollen then drops from the pistil onto the ovary.
Fertilization occurs, and an apple begins to grow. Part of
the ovary will become the apple core and seeds, while the
ovary's outer wall will develop into the apple's flesh.

developing
apple

Young apples grow throughout the summer. They are nourished by sugars made in the leaves through a process called photosynthesis. It takes fifty leaves to feed one apple!

In midsummer orchard workers remove small or misshapen fruit. Only the best apples are left to mature.

Two weeks before harvest apples no longer need food from their leaves. Instead they make their own food by changing the starch in their flesh into sugar. This sugar, along with bright sunlight, causes a chemical reaction in the cells of the apples' skin. The reaction creates a pigment that determines the apples' color. By harvesttime apples glow dark red, pink, orange, yellow, and green, or even a mixture of all of these colors. Apples can be striped, splotched, or spotted.

Harvest is a time for celebration, but it is a time for hard work, too. The best fruit is handpicked before it can fall to the ground and bruise. Fruits that are damaged are made into apple juice, applesauce, and other apple products. Only about sixty percent of the apple crop is eaten fresh.

Ripe apples are carefully placed in huge wooden bins. When full, the bins are taken to enormous refrigerated warehouses. There the apples are washed and sorted for color, size, and quality. Sorted apples are repacked into smaller bushel boxes, each weighing about forty-two pounds. Finally refrigerated trains and trucks transport the apples to processing plants or grocery stores.

Varieties

Thousands of apple varieties are grown in the United States, and each one has its own special qualities. Some apples grow to the size of a cherry, while others grow as big as a grapefruit. Here are a few varieties that you might want to try. Which is your favorite?

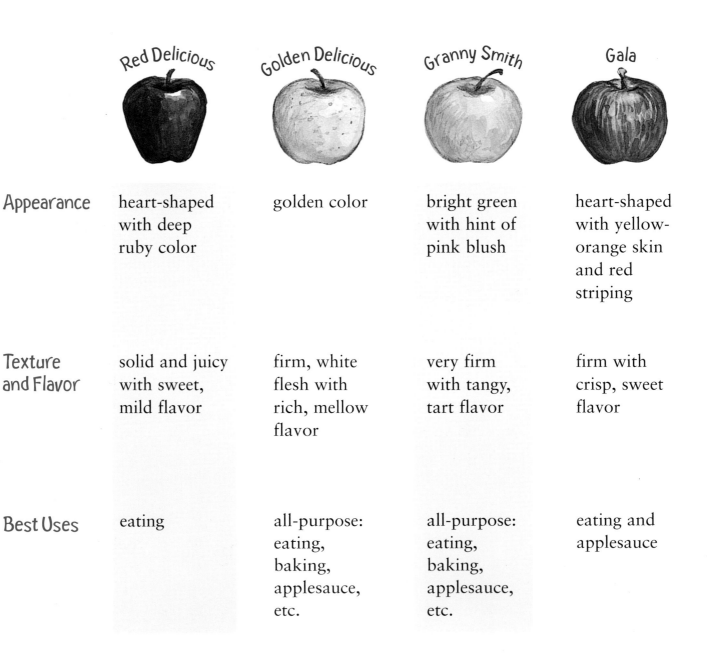

	Red Delicious	Golden Delicious	Granny Smith	Gala
Appearance	heart-shaped with deep ruby color	golden color	bright green with hint of pink blush	heart-shaped with yellow-orange skin and red striping
Texture and Flavor	solid and juicy with sweet, mild flavor	firm, white flesh with rich, mellow flavor	very firm with tangy, tart flavor	firm with crisp, sweet flavor
Best Uses	eating	all-purpose: eating, baking, applesauce, etc.	all-purpose: eating, baking, applesauce, etc.	eating and applesauce

Fuji	McIntosh	Pink Lady	Rome Beauty

color varies: yellow-green with hint of red to very red	mixture of red and green coloring	pink blush over yellow	bright red and red-striped skin
firm with spicy, crisp, sweet flavor	soft, juicy, and fine texture with crisp, tart, tender flavor	firm with sweet-tart flavor	crisp with medium tart to sweet flavor
eating, pie making, baking, and applesauce	excellent for eating	excellent for eating and applesauce	baking and cooking

Colonial Cider Press

Apple cider

In Colonial times apple cider was the most common drink. It continued to be the most common fruit drink until the 1930s.

In the cider mill apples are sorted and washed. Most cider makers have a secret mix of apple varieties that they think will make their cider taste special. Clean apples are chopped and put in a huge apple press. The apples are then squeezed with over one thousand pounds of pressure. The result is raw apple juice called cider.

Occasionally freshly pressed cider may contain harmful bacteria that can make you sick. For safety's sake it's best to drink pasteurized cider. Pasteurization is the process of heating juice to 160 degrees Fahrenheit in order to kill germs. Cider needs constant refrigeration.

Apple cider is different from apple juice. Apple juice is raw juice that has been filtered twice, pasteurized, and vacuum sealed so that it stays fresh without refrigeration until opened.

Nutrition

The average American eats about sixty-five fresh apples each year. Most of us eat over twenty pounds of applesauce. Of course, we all love apple pie. Apples provide many of the nutrients we need to be healthy.

An apple eaten with the skin on is best for you. Almost half of an apple's vitamin C is just under the skin. Apples are also high in fiber and vitamins, which can help keep your heart healthy and may even help prevent certain kinds of cancer.

A medium apple has only eighty calories, no sodium, and no fat. Eating an apple will clean the teeth, sweeten the breath, and massage the gums. Some people call the apple "nature's toothbrush."

Tips

Apples should be stored in the refrigerator. If left on the kitchen counter, they can get mushy in just two or three days.

Apples need to be carefully washed before cooking or eating them. Washing apples helps people avoid exposure to insecticides and germs. Even the slice of a knife into an unwashed piece of fruit can carry insecticide into the fruit's flesh. Organic farmers use fewer pesticides, making organic apples a healthier choice.

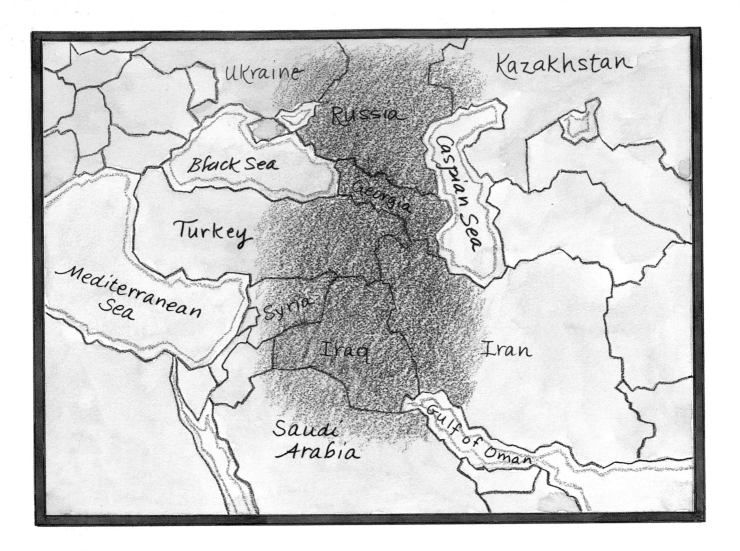

Apple history

Wild apples, called crab apples, have existed for thousands of years. They are small, sour, and full of brown seeds. As early as the Stone Age, people worked to improve the crab apple's taste.

Most apple historians believe that sweet apples were first cultivated in Southwest and Central Asia around 6500 BCE.

During the Greek and Roman Empires, farmers learned how to grow apples that were sweeter and crisper than any before them. By the 7th century BCE, the Greeks had cultivated several types of sweet apples. Later, during the Roman Empire, historian Pliny the Elder recorded that Roman farmers had developed thirty-seven new varieties of apples.

The Romans even had a goddess of fruit trees named Pomona. Today the science of growing apples and other fruit is called pomology.

The Greeks believed that the apple represented love and beauty. In ancient Greece tossing an apple to a girl was a marriage proposal. If she caught it the answer was yes!

Romans also thought that the apple was a symbol of love and romance. After they invaded Britain they happily adopted the British custom of bobbing for apples. Apples were floated in a tub of water, and young, unmarried people would try to bite into one. The Romans believed that the first to come up with an apple in his or her mouth would be the first to marry in the coming year.

The word "apple" probably came from the Old English word *aeppel*, which referred to all fruit. The first printed reference to the word "apple" appeared in a book written in the 1200s by an English monk named Bartholomew. As time passed the word "apple" came to mean the fruit as we know it today.

The use of apples in stories and folklore is common. One of the most famous is the folktale of William Tell.

Legend says that in 1307 Swiss archer William Tell was arrested for failing to bow before the hat of the German governor. As punishment the governor had Tell's son tied to a tree and ordered Tell to shoot an apple off his son's head. If Tell refused, his son would be killed. Tell was famous for his skill with a crossbow, and, fortunately, his aim was good. He split the apple neatly in half and saved his son's life.

When the Mayflower Pilgrims arrived in America, they were disappointed to find that crab apples were the only apples growing in their new home. They discovered that the native bees, unlike Europe's honeybees, did a poor job of pollinating the apple trees' flowers. Within a year hives of honeybees were brought from England so that apple cultivation in the colonies could begin.

It was not until 1629 that the first large shipment of seeds and seedlings arrived in America under the care of John Endicott, an early governor of the Massachusetts Bay Colony. Historians say that Endicott planted the first apple orchard in the Americas in 1630.

By the late 1700s missionaries, traders, and Native Americans headed west. The most famous of these was a missionary named John Chapman, who was born in Leominster, Massachusetts, in 1775.

Chapman, eventually known as Johnny Appleseed, set out for the West in 1797. Often seen barefoot, he wore his cooking pan as a hat and a potato sack with holes cut for his head and arms as a shirt. This odd-looking man was a gentle person, a preacher, and a gardener who simply wanted to help people have enough food to eat.

Johnny Appleseed did not just scatter apple seeds, as many people once thought. Using seeds from Pennsylvania cider mills, he planted many apple orchards in the Midwest. Each year he would return to check on his trees. He kept at his work for forty years.

Apples were considered necessary for good health, and in the 1800s a law was passed that required homesteaders to plant orchards of fifty apple trees on their land. Travelers on the Oregon Trail were known to carry apple seedlings in their covered wagons. These settlers often planted their orchard before building their house! Today the Pacific Northwest is one of the largest apple-growing areas in the country.

Baking and eating fresh apple pie is one of the rewards of apple season.

Traditional Apple Pie

With an adult's help, preheat the oven to 400° F.

Ingredients:

1 package ready-made piecrust (in the dairy case of the grocery store)

6 cooking apples such as Granny Smith or Golden Delicious, thoroughly washed

1 tablespoon lemon juice

½ cup sugar

¼ cup flour

¼ cup packed brown sugar

1 teaspoon cinnamon

¼ teaspoon nutmeg

1 tablespoon cold butter

1 egg

salt

Procedure:

Line a 9-inch pie plate with one of the piecrusts.

Peel, core, and slice the apples. Place the apples in a large bowl and toss them with the lemon juice. Combine the sugar, flour, brown sugar, cinnamon, and nutmeg, and add this mixture to the apples. Toss until the apples are completely coated. Cut the cold butter into small cubes and add them to the apple mixture.

Pour the apples into the lined pie plate, piling them high in the center. Top with the second piecrust and pinch the edges to seal. Cut slits in the piecrust to allow steam to escape.

Beat an egg and add a pinch of salt. Brush this mixture over the top crust. Cover the pie loosely with foil to prevent over-browning. Bake for 30 minutes. Remove foil and bake 30 minutes more, or until apples are tender.

Apple Facts and Records

 October is National Apple Month.

 According to the *Guinness Book of World Records,* the largest known apple weighed 3.2 pounds.

The world's longest apple peel, 172 feet 4 inches long, was carved by Kathy Wafler Madison on October 16, 1976.

 Twenty-five percent of an apple's volume is air. That is why it floats.

More than 7,500 varieties of apples are grown around the world.

China grows 41 percent of all apples, making it the leading producer of apples in the world.

The United States is the second largest apple producer. The states of New York, Pennsylvania, Virginia, Michigan, and Washington are the biggest producers in the United States.

 President John Adams drank a pitcher of apple cider every morning and credited it for his long life. He died at the age of 90.

The American colonists called the apple a "winter banana" or a "melt-in-the-mouth."

 Native Americans who had never seen honeybees before, called them the "white man's flies."

Isaac Newton is said to have come up with the Universal Law of Gravitation as he reflected on an apple falling from a tree.

 In 400 BCE Hippocrates, the father of medicine, believed in natural remedies. Apples were one of his favorite "prescriptions."

Resources

If you want to learn more about apples, check out these resources:

Gibbons, Gail. *Apples.* New York: Holiday House, 2000.

Johnson, Sylvia A. *Apple Trees.* Minneapolis, MN: Lerner Publications, 1983.

Maestro, Betsy. *How Do Apples Grow?* New York: HarperCollins, 1992.

Robbins, Ken. *Apples.* New York: Atheneum Books for Young Readers, 2002.

Wolfman, Judy. *Life on an Apple Orchard.* Minneapolis, MN: Carolrhoda Books, 2004.

Washington Apples
www.bestapples.com
Find out what it is like to live on an apple orchard. This website also features apple trivia, apple recipes, and apple activities.

To Kevin, the apple of my eye
—J. F.

To Stacy and Jeff, two apples of my eye
—P. L. T.

Text copyright © 2007 by Jacqueline Farmer
Illustrations copyright © 2007 by Phyllis Limbacher Tildes
All rights reserved, including the right of reproduction in whole or in part in any form.
Charlesbridge and colophon are registered trademarks of Charlesbridge Publishing, Inc.

Published by Charlesbridge
85 Main Street
Watertown, MA 02472
(617) 926-0329
www.charlesbridge.com

Library of Congress Cataloging-in-Publication Data
Farmer, Jacqueline.
    Apples / Jacqueline Farmer ; illustrated by Phyllis Limbacher Tildes.
       p.   cm.
    ISBN: 978-1-57091-694-6 (reinforced for library use)
    ISBN: 978-1-57091-695-3 (softcover)
1. Apples—Juvenile literature. I. Tildes, Phyllis Limbacher. II. Title.
SB363.F27 2007
634'.11—dc22   2006020942

Printed in Korea
(hc) 10 9 8 7 6 5 4 3 2 1
(sc) 10 9 8 7 6 5 4 3 2 1

Illustrations done in watercolor and pencil on illustration board
Display type and text type set in Ogre and Sabon
Color separations by Chroma Graphics, Singapore
Printed and bound by Sung In Printing, South Korea
Production supervision by Brian G. Walker
Designed by Diane M. Earley